Original title:
The Colors of Love

Copyright © 2024 Creative Arts Management OÜ
All rights reserved.

Author: Daniel Brooks
ISBN HARDBACK: 978-9908-0-0490-7
ISBN PAPERBACK: 978-9908-0-0491-4

Origins of Love in Aquamarine

In a sea of jellybeans, we met,
Your blue was like the ocean's pet.
I tripped on marshmallows, what a sight,
You laughed so hard, it felt just right.

Our hearts did sail on candy tides,
With gummy dolphins as our guides.
We danced on waves of fizzy drink,
And shared our dreams in lemon ink.

Flickering Lanterns of Connection

At a quirky fair, we spun around,
Your laughter echoed, a joyful sound.
We chased those lights in the wishing glow,
Tripped on fortune cookies, oh what a show!

With every spark, my heart did race,
You threw a pie, it hit my face.
We donned those hats that made us twirl,
In this silly world, you are my pearl.

Portraits in Vivid Sentiment

You painted hearts with ketchup flair,
A masterpiece beyond compare.
Your smile's the brush, my heart's the canvas,
Together, we make a lovely madness.

We strut like ducks in polka dot,
With silly poses in every spot.
Oh, how we laugh at our strange art,
Each stroke a quirk, each beat a heart.

Fragrant Blooms of Enchanted Love

In a garden filled with which led scent,
You plucked a rose, oh, what a event!
But bees were buzzing, so we dashed,
Champagne on daisies, our laughter splashed.

We wrapped ourselves in petals bright,
In butterfly glasses, what a sight!
With every sniff, the world turns sweet,
In this flower field, our hearts do meet.

Sunlit Promises in Pastel

In a world where hues compete,
I painted you a love so sweet.
Your socks are pink, your shirt's a green,
Our fashion choices? A funny scene.

A dance with shades of lightened glee,
You wore that hat; it looked like tea!
We twirled in taffy, spun in cheer,
Laughing at our rainbow sphere.

Umbrella's broken, love's in bloom,
We color outside every room.
Our laughter echoes, bright and clear,
Making every moment dear!

The Richness of Burgundy Yearnings

You poured the wine, I spilled the drink,
A necklace made of grapes, don't blink!
Your eyes are deep like wine's delight,
  Where each sip leads to silly flight.

With burgundy dreams, we toast the night,
But tripped on shoes, oh what a sight!
We clinked our glasses with a cheer,
While glancing at the shimm'ring beer.

Romantic dinners take a twist,
We cook and burn, oh can't resist!
The richness here is clear to see,
Can you make the peas less green, maybe?

Vibrance of a Heart Unfurled

In gardens bright where laughter grows,
A vibrant heart sways, everyone knows.
You wore those pants so loud and bold,
Flip-flops squeaked with tales untold.

With every step, a comic scene,
A tumble here, a wink so keen.
Our vibrant love is like a kite,
Sailing high, oh what a sight!

We're splattered with paint, but who cares?
I smile wide, and my heart flares.
As long as you trip, I'll laugh in glee,
Together, love, we're a silly spree!

Whimsical Blooms of Togetherness

In a garden where the giggles grow,
We laugh so hard, the flowers glow.
You planted daisies with a twist,
Their faces smile, can't be dismissed.

Whimsical blooms, sprouting here and there,
Look at that bee—it's in your hair!
With petals flying, love's a breeze,
In a world of fun, we do as we please.

We prance like rabbits, fluffed and bright,
Dancing to a tune of pure delight.
Each bloom a laugh, each laugh a dance,
Our whimsical love, in every glance!

Palette of Passionate Dreams

In a land where socks don't match,
He painted hearts with silly patch!
With a brush dipped in a swirl of cheer,
He spun a tale of laughter here.

On purple skies where cupcakes dance,
He found a muse, so bold by chance.
With rainbow sprinkles on her cake,
They shared a joy, for friendship's sake.

A tangerine cat sang a tune,
While they both waltzed 'neath a silver moon.
His red balloon floated high in glee,
Giggling, she chased it, wild and free.

With hues of green, they made a mess,
A splash of joy, a proud, sweet dress.
In every brush stroke, they would find,
A world full of love, so sweet and kind.

Hues of Affection's Embrace

In a yellow hat, he told a joke,
While juggling oranges, he almost choked.
She wore a smile, like lipstick red,
As laughter melted all her dread.

With crayons bright, they drew their dreams,
In wiggly lines and funny themes.
Blue elephants danced with pink skates,
Creating giggles that never fades.

He tripped on green grass, a little clumsy,
While she snorted, her giggles so chummy.
A purple dog barked a silly tune,
As love bloomed bright like a cartoon.

Amidst the chaos, they'd find a rhyme,
Spinning in joy, lost track of time.
With every chuckle, their hearts took flight,
Painting a world, dazzling and bright.

The Spectrum of Heartstrings

With crayons wide, they sketched the day,
In mismatched socks, they'd laugh and play.
Bouncing hearts on a pogo stick,
Their silly antics, a joyful trick.

A chartreuse frog croaked a quick rhyme,
As they twirled together, defying time.
With every hug, the colors shone,
Crafting a bond that felt like home.

His tie-dye shirt became a cape,
While her giggles weaved a funny tape.
In a canvas world of wild delight,
Their love was a rainbow, shining bright.

With sparkles tossed in the air around,
They danced through fields, their joy unbound.
In a whimsical world where laughter stayed,
Their hearts painted sunsets that never fade.

Shades of Infinite Longing

On a canvas wide, where dreams collide,
He painted hints of love and pride.
With a polka-dot brush, so misaligned,
He crafted moments that felt divine.

A cerulean dog tried to ride a bike,
While she laughed and took a giant hike.
In splashes of joy, they found their way,
In puddles of color, they'd laugh and play.

With sticky fingers and cake on their face,
They turned the kitchen into a wild space.
As the whisk twirled in a messy spin,
They brewed up fun, letting love win!

As twilight crept on the painted sky,
They lay back laughing, just you and I.
In every shade of their joyous plight,
They found their colors in pure delight.

Shadows of True Intimacy

In the dark, we tango, my foot finds the chair,
You laugh as we stumble, it's love in mid-air.
I swear I'm more graceful, just give me some wine,
But there's a clear shadow, and it's not just my spine.

Your socks are mismatched, a riot of hues,
Each step feels like dancing with one of my shoes.
We snort when we giggle, like balloons filled with air,
Who knew that true love comes with such flair?

Glistening Glimpses of Joy

Baking together, flour flies like a spree,
You taste all the batter, I'm left with the spree.
The cake rises slowly, a lopsided delight,
We toss sprinkles with laughter, oh what a sight!

You take a big bite, then I plant a sweet kiss,
Your frosting-filled cheeks look like an icing abyss.
We smile through the chaos, with chocolatey glee,
In this fun kitchen dance, it's just you and me.

The Harmony of Chromatic Caresses

Your hug is a mixture of pickles and jam,
A curious combo, but still, I think 'damn!'
We twirl like two dervishes, lost in the mix,
Each squeeze, every giggle, pure love in the fix.

We paint with our laughter, in shades very bright,
Throwing splashes of humor, a wild festive sight.
Like rainbows on ice cream, we blend and collide,
With you, my dear partner, I've got nothing to hide.

Sapphire Skies Over Cherry Blossoms

Under blue skies we tiptoe, in clumsy parade,
Each blossom we crush, it feels like we've played.
You giggle at petals, they fall like rain,
I swear they're just laughing, it's quite insane!

Your hair gets caught, and the wind starts to tease,
We chase all the petals just like a wild breeze.
With a wink and a chuckle, we spin and we sway,
Who knew spring's a dance, come what may?

Canvas of Serene Embraces

On a canvas bright, I paint my cheer,
With splatters of laughter, never a tear.
A brushstroke of giggles, a swirl of delight,
In this masterpiece, everything feels right.

A polka-dotted heart, oh what a sight,
With balloons of joy, I'm flying so high.
Every color a quirk, every shade a rhyme,
Creating this artwork, one giggle at a time.

Mesmerizing Patterns of Heartfelt Reality

In a garden of whimsy, blooms all around,
Each petal a chuckle, joy unbound.
Daisies in tutus, dancing in glee,
The bees wear sunglasses, sipping their tea.

A sun that winks with a cheeky grin,
While clouds do the cha-cha, let the fun begin!
In this colorful chaos, we find our groove,
With vibrant vibrations, let's shimmy and move.

The Subtlety of Crimson Greetings

With a wink of a rose, I send you cheer,
A shrubbery grin that tickles the ear.
Rustling leaves giggle, from a breeze so bright,
Whispering secrets of silly delight.

Roses wear bows, tulips don hats,
Laughing at lovers and all their spats.
In a splash of red, I send you my jest,
A bouquet of chuckles, consider it a quest!

Harmonizing with the Tones of Affection

Join me in this tune, a merry prank,
With harmonies twinkling, in love's full rank.
The accordion's wheeze makes us all sway,
As we jive with delight, come what may.

The xylophone chimes, each note a tease,
Tickling your heart like a sweet summer breeze.
Together we'll dance, in this jubilee,
With laughter as our partner, wild and free!

Ethereal Echoes

In a world of pastel skies,
He wore socks with polka dots,
She danced in a tulle disguise,
Giggles echoed, like happy thoughts.

A pie made of rainbow hues,
Flavors clashed, what a fuss!
Blueberry meets pickle juice,
A taste that gave everyone a rush.

He painted smiles on the wall,
With mustard and jelly too,
The house a canvas, quite a ball,
Laughter and chaos in every hue.

So grab your brush, join the spree,
Paint the day with silly flair,
For joy in colors, wild and free,
Brings grins that float in the air.

Vibrant Threads

A sweater knit from laughter's thread,
Each stitch a giggle, oh so bright,
He wore it proudly, but instead,
It smelled like socks left out at night.

She knitted hats in yellow stripes,
He paired them with his moonlight pants,
Their wardrobe? Hilarious types,
The fashion show, a clumsy dance.

With mismatched shoes and joyful grins,
They strutted through town, hand in hand,
Accidental twirls, laughter spins,
A silly, vibrant, wacky band.

In a tapestry of goofy dreams,
Threads that tangle but never break,
Each vibrant laugh, a little beam,
Of love, the sweetest kind of make.

Celestial Affinity

Starry eyes met in mid-air,
With a comet made of fluffy cheese,
She asked, 'Is that your cosmic hair?'
He grinned, 'It's my favorite tease!'

Under moons of popcorn white,
They danced on clouds of candy floss,
Floating high, what a sight,
Their love was both sweet and loss.

Galaxies spun with silly grace,
As aliens tried to join the fun,
With three eyes and a dancing face,
They laughed until the stars all run.

In this universe, bright and weird,
They twirled like planets, round and round,
With every chuckle, love appeared,
In cosmic humor, joy is found.

Lush Landscapes of the Heart

In a garden where daisies sway,
She planted gnomes with silly hats,
He painted tulips in bright array,
While chasing after puppy spats.

Their veggies wore expressive crowns,
With carrots dancing, peas that prance,
In laughter, they'd forget the frowns,
And grow a love that loves to dance.

With sunflowers sporting grins so wide,
They played hide-and-seek with the bees,
A picnic under trees, full of pride,
Included pies and tickles, if you please.

In landscapes lush and hearts so keen,
They laughed through every bumpy part,
For love, as bright as grass so green,
Flourishes best within the heart.

Tidal Waves of Coral Hues

In a world of sweets and treats,
A crush felt like sticky beets.
You winked, I tripped on my own shoe,
Who knew love made me so askew?

You wore a tie that clashed with red,
Yet somehow, my heart you wed.
Each laugh a splash of bright young love,
Like jellyfish dancing from above.

Twilight Tints of Connection

Underneath a sky so blue,
We shared a soda, then we flew.
Your hair got stuck in my cotton candy,
And suddenly, our giggles grew dandy!

You said my dance was purely grand,
While stepping on toes was not the plan.
But oh, in colors so absurd,
Our mismatched hearts just flipped and stirred.

The Glimmer of Emerald Affection

Your eyes sparkled like a fountain,
I fell for you near a mountain.
You joked of fish and lopsided hats,
Our silly talks turned into spats.

In a sea of green, we took a chance,
Dancing like we didn't care to prance.
Amidst the giggles and happy sighs,
Our love grew taller than the skies.

Whispered Wishes in Charcoal

In shadows deep, we found our spark,
Your laugh echoed in the dark.
With crayon hearts drawn on the walls,
We made up games and silly calls.

You wore socks that always mismatch,
But that's what made our hearts attach.
Whispers turned to giggles light,
With charcoal dreams, we took our flight.

Daring Delights

In a land where giggles bloom,
Cats and dogs share the room.
Hearts in shades of silly red,
Dance with joy, oh what a spread!

Chocolate kisses melt away,
While marshmallow clouds play the day.
Bubblegum laughter fills the air,
Love's a circus, if you dare!

Socks mismatched, yet oh so bright,
Kite-flying in the sun's delight.
With ice cream dripping down your chin,
A chuckle's the sweetest thing to win!

So let's paint our world with cheer,
Tickle fights are drawing near.
Love's a game of silly pranks,
Join the fun, let's raise our thanks!

Radiant Essence

Dancing under disco lights,
Love's a party, with no fights.
In polka dots and funky shoes,
Every turn's a joyful muse!

Confetti hearts fall from the sky,
As laughter makes the moments fly.
Puppies in tutus twirl around,
Chasing dreams on giggle ground!

Chocolate mustaches on our lips,
Silly dances, goofy flips.
With balloons shaped like our dreams,
Life's a wild ride, bursting seams!

So wear your smiles, bright like gems,
Skip and hop with all your friends.
In this realm where joy's the theme,
Love is laughter—we all scream!

Whispers of Crimson Hearts

A love note scribbled on a napkin,
Promises wrapped in playful grin.
Funny faces, silly glares,
Flickering candles, love declares!

We dance like jellybeans in a jar,
Twisting and turning, oh so bizarre.
With each step, a giggle burst,
In this quirky love, we're immersed!

Puns and jokes are our sweet glue,
Sticking us tight, just me and you.
Throwing sprinkles on each other's heads,
Rolling in laughter, love spreads!

Let's wear capes and fly real high,
Making wishes as clouds drift by.
In this wacky world, we play our part,
Every laugh's a beat in our heart!

Echoes in the Lavender Twilight

Lavender skies, with stars that wink,
As we laugh and share a drink.
Ticklish whispers in the night,
Every moment feels just right!

Silly serenades in the park,
Where every dog joins in with a bark.
Floating lanterns of love's charm,
In this madness, we're all warm!

Kites that tangle, oh what a sight,
Twirling around in sheer delight.
Cactus hugs and daisy chains,
In this garden, silliness reigns!

So let's toast with soda pop,
To the joy that never stops.
In echoes bright, together we sway,
Love's fun ride, come what may!

Subtle Gradations

In the kitchen, red beets dive,
Cooking dinner, alive with jive.
He spills the sauce, it splatters bold,
On my shirt, a masterpiece told.

Green spinach adds to dinner's flair,
But the dog thinks it's a new fair share.
Gathering veggies, oh what a sight,
He wears an apron, I start to bite.

Blueberries roll around the floor,
As we laugh, can't take it anymore.
In the chaos, there's joy to find,
In these little things, hearts entwined.

With each mishap, we giggle and cheer,
Love's in the laughter, so loud and clear.
Fruits of our labor, messy but sweet,
A family feast, it's quite the treat.

Cascading Cares

The sun splashes yellow on the grass,
Silly shadows dance as moments pass.
We trip on daisies, start to laugh,
Counting giggles, it's our craft.

With a wink, the clouds wear gray,
A burst of thunder has come to play.
Dashing inside with all our might,
Holding hands, it feels just right.

In the puddles, we jump with glee,
Making rainbows from what we see.
Each splash a smile, so carefree,
Turning storms into joy, just you and me.

With every color, every parade,
A canvas of chaos, memories made.
In this tapestry, we truly shine,
With heart and laughter, all intertwined.

Warmth of Unity

Crisp mornings bring pumpkin spice cheer,
We sip our drinks, a toast to the year.
Two mugs clinking, a warming sound,
In cozy corners, love's found around.

Snuggled in blankets, we exchange dreams,
Navigating life's funny extremes.
One sock here, and one sock there,
Laughter echoes, floating in air.

Let's bake a cake, a colorful mess,
Measuring love, who'd dare to guess?
Frosting everywhere, a sticky fight,
Who knew in chaos, we'd find delight?

As we clean up, we giggle and tease,
Life's sweeter moments are sure to please.
With sprinkles of joy, and crumbs to share,
Unity shines, with laughter in the air.

Refreshing Rainbows

Colorful socks on laundry day,
With a twist and a turn, they find their way.
A mismatched dance on the bedroom floor,
Each shade a giggle, who could want more?

We paint the walls in wild tones,
But sprinkles fall, oh my, the groans.
In turquoise mess, we find our bliss,
For every dot, we steal a kiss.

Through every splash, we poke some fun,
Inventing shades, the blending's begun.
A palette of joy across our lives,
In clumsy strokes, affection thrives.

And when the sun breaks after the rain,
Each color glows, erasing the pain.
With splashes of joy, we dare to play,
In our funny world, love leads the way.

Cerulean Serenades of Desire

In skies of blue, the heart takes flight,
A wink exchanged under moon's soft light.
With every laugh, the spark ignites,
In playful banter, love delight.

Dancing gaily on a sandy shore,
Chasing waves, we crave for more.
Splashing water, oh what a sight,
You stole my heart, I hope you don't bite!

With ice cream cones that melt away,
Sharing sticky smiles on this sweet day.
A rollercoaster of whimsy and cheer,
You make the world so bright and clear.

As cerulean dreams take on their form,
We navigate each twist and norm.
Hand in hand, like petals in spring,
You are my laugh, my everything!

Golden Threads of Connection

In a world of gold, we seem to shine,
With silly jokes, your hand in mine.
You trip on air, I laugh so loud,
Together we sway, a dancing crowd.

Like buttered toast with honey spread,
You're my snack, enough said!
We laugh at stains on our favorite shirts,
Finding joy in all the quirks.

In the kitchen, a culinary spree,
Burnt toast and laughter just you and me.
With clumsy charm, we create a mess,
Yet every bite is filled with zest.

A golden sunbeam on this fine day,
We chase ambitions, come what may.
For silly moments, we always strive,
In this ridiculous dance we thrive!

Tapestry of Fleeting Emotions

A patchwork quilt of quirky feels,
We stitch together with our squeals.
Each thread a story, some bright, some dim,
But always a laugh, never a whim.

Like kittens tangled in a ball of yarn,
Playful chaos is our charm.
Through ups and downs, we twirl and spin,
Finding joy even when we grin.

With fleeting moments that come and go,
We sing off-key, but let love flow.
A recipe of giggles with a sprinkle of grace,
In this madcap waltz, we've found our place.

In the tapestry of our tangled hearts,
Every quirk is where the fun starts.
So let's weave tales with a twist and shout,
For in laughter, there's never a doubt!

Silken Moments in Rose

In fragrant blooms our laughter thrives,
With silk and petals, our hearts arrive.
You trip over roses, and I can't help but grin,
This fragrant chaos is where love begins.

A tea party set for two in delight,
Spilling sugar, what a sweet sight!
With each sip, your face turns bright,
A rosy moment, just feels so right.

In sunlit meadows, we leap and spin,
Chasing butterflies, letting fun in.
Every tumble brings us closer still,
In a garden of laughter, we find our thrill.

When silken moments in bloom unfold,
We weave our stories, tender and bold.
With petals in hair and joy in our eyes,
In a world so whimsical, our love always flies!

Symphony of Sable and Silk

In a tuxedo made of furs,
Dancing with my pet goldfish,
We waltz on a slippery deck,
His bow tie's a little too swish.

A red sock in a sea of blue,
I wore it out to mischief's call,
It danced with my wacky shoe,
Whirling like a nutty ball.

Under stars with fake mustaches,
We serenade the glowing moon,
A laughter fit for hundred crashes,
Who knew love could feel like a cartoon?

With spaghetti hanging on our ears,
We glance at pasta's twirly threat,
In each bite, we conquer fears,
Love's a feast we won't forget.

Chromatic Embrace

A jester hat of neon light,
I'm dizzy from the spin of hues,
You threw sprinkles in the night,
And laughter lit the skies like blues.

Chasing cupcakes made of rain,
You slipped on icing, what a sight,
Fell into a whipped cream lane,
Now you're a tasty, frosted knight.

Your words are candy-coated lies,
I giggle as you trip and stumble,
In this dance, we improvise,
Our hearts beat, silly and humble.

On roller skates of jellybean,
We glide through love's sticky spree,
With every tumble, we're more keen,
This wacky ride is pure glee!

Vivid Whispers

A parrot sings in technicolor,
Tales of socks lost in the dryer,
You laugh while tripping on the floor,
In this antics-filled empire.

Your hat is shaped like a big slice,
Of pizza topped with cheesy glee,
Each look exchanged feels like a heist,
We steal smiles, just you and me.

Jumping puddles filled with ink,
We paint each other with delight,
While shaking up the cosmic stink,
Laughter wins this playful fight.

With crayons drawn on city walls,
Our doodles dance in wild delight,
In this world, nothing restrains,
Every sketch turns wrongs to right.

Radiance of Desire

A disco ball in the kitchen,
Reflecting moments bright and rare,
We swirl around like kittens,
Caught in tango without a care.

Your socks are misfits, I can see,
One's striped while the other's polka dot,
Yet you dance like you're fancy-free,
In love's rhythm, we lose the plot.

A quiche shaped like a cartoon cat,
You served it with a wink and a wink,
We feasted till we couldn't chat,
Our giggles, the food's missing link.

Love's a treasure, odd and bright,
With quirky gems and things askew,
It fills our days with pure delight,
In silly shades, just me and you.

Tints of Tenderness and Light

A wink of pink, you make me grin,
Your laughter sparkles, where do I begin?
Yellow shoes and polka-dot ties,
We dance like we're clowns under a sky full of pies.

A dash of blue when you steal my fries,
We argue like kids, what a sweet surprise!
With snacks all around, our love's a buffet,
Who knew fun could get this gourmet?

Your fuchsia face when I tickle your knee,
We're two silly ducks, quacking with glee.
Let's paint our days with a splash of good cheer,
In this wild, vivid world, you're the color I'll steer.

As orange sunsets fade into night,
We giggle and snort, what a hilarious sight!
With crayons in hand, we sketch our delight,
In love's joyful realm, everything feels right.

A Canvas of Celestial Affection

On the canvas, we splatter with bright sticky glue,
Laughing like children, what a colorful crew!
With each silly stroke, we shade in our dreams,
Creating a masterpiece bursting at the seams.

Your purple smudge on my nose makes me smile,
We paint silly portraits, each one unique style.
With brushes a-wobble, we reach for the sky,
Dancing with colors that never run dry.

An orange burst when you say I'm the best,
In this art studio, we've put love to the test.
Each stroke is a giggle, a laugh, and a cheer,
In the gallery of life, you're my best souvenir.

Twirling 'round crazily in paint-splattered shoes,
Our hearts beat like drums in hues we can't lose.
With every wild splash, we revel and sway,
In this joyful chaos, let's splash our love play!

The Graphite of Resilient Bonds

In doodles of graphite, we sketch out our tale,
With each silly scribble, we purposely fail.
Yet laughter erupts with each quirky mistake,
In this graphite dance, our hearts nearly shake.

You draw a big heart that bends and breaks too,
We giggle and chuckle, oh, what will we do?
Your stick figure eyebrows arch high with delight,
In this wobbly world, love makes it feel right.

We shade in our joys with the silliest flair,
A comic strip life with laughs we can share.
In circles and squiggles, our moments take flight,
As we sketch out the fun, in black and white light.

So let's doodle our dreams on this canvas so fine,
With messes and giggles, we know they'll align.
Our bond is a drawing that never goes flat,
In every sharp pencil, there's love in the chat!

Brushstrokes of Enchanted Moments

Brushstrokes of whimsy, we dash and we swirl,
With splashes of laughter, our hearts start to twirl.
A squeeze of the brush, a tickle of fate,
In this artful venture, we never feel late.

You spill the paint, and I shout with glee,
What a masterpiece! Come, let's just be free!
Canvas of chaos, where giggles emerge,
In this swirling ballet, we're ready to surge.

The palette of joy, oh, how brightly it glows,
With blues of the sky and pinks like a rose.
Every moment we share, like paint that won't dry,
In the gallery of giggles, we always comply.

As the colors collide, we feel so alive,
In love's art studio, our spirits will thrive.
With brushes in hand, we shall write our own song,
Forever creating, where laughter belongs.

Dances in Sunlit Marigold

In fields of bright and bustling hue,
A dance of bees with honeydew.
The flowers wink, their petals sway,
As laughter blooms throughout the day.

A dandelion in a tuxedo fine,
Declares its love for that bright wine.
The clumsy ants do tango small,
In sunflower courts, they trip and fall.

The Infinite Shades of Shared Smiles

With every grin, a twinkle glows,
Like jellybeans in a conga row.
The piquant taste of gummy cheer,
Makes friendship sweet, oh my, my dear!

Popcorn clouds in skies of joy,
Bouncing 'round like a playful toy.
In every chuckle, a rainbow's spun,
As giggles sneak away and run.

Radiating Warmth of Golden Gleams

With sunny rays that tickle toes,
And warmth that dances, goodness grows.
A buttercup crowns a playful head,
While sunshine sprinkles sleepy dread.

Silly squirrels in a game of tag,
Chasing shadows, never a drag.
They leap and bound on branches wide,
In this bright world, they take their pride.

Life in a Rainbow's Embrace

In splashes bright, the world does sing,
Where jellyfish wear a jeweled ring.
A clash of hues, a vibrant show,
As laughter paints the cheeky glow.

Marshmallow clouds float soft and sweet,
While candy-hued rain drips a treat.
The playful wind in colors twirls,
As happiness unfurls and whirls.

A Rosie Glow of Dreamy Whispers

In a garden of giggles, hearts take flight,
Roses blush pink, not too bright.
With each silly wink, the petals sway,
Whispering secrets in a playful way.

Butterflies dance in a humorous spree,
Tickled by pollen, oh what glee!
A daisy winks, saying, 'You're cute!'
While the sunflowers jest, 'Don't be a brute!'

Laughter echoes, a sweet serenade,
With each poke-nudge, a funny charade.
In this patch of joy, love's just a game,
Where even the thorns wear a smile, not shame.

The Symphony of Light and Desire

Under the moon, we play the fool,
Twinkling stars burst in a sparkling pool.
Each glance a note in a humorous score,
Dancing under beams, who could ask for more?

With laughter erupting like a comedic song,
The rhythm of hearts is wonderfully wrong.
A trumpet of giggles, a cymbal's delight,
As we tango in shadows, oh what a sight!

A maestro of puns leads the bright show,
Each joke a crescendo, and on we go.
In this ball of mirth, we twirl and we spin,
With love just a quirk, it's where we begin.

Indigo Vows Beneath the Stars

In twilight's embrace, we craft our decree,
With promises tied like bright blue spaghetti.
Each word a giggle, each laugh a charm,
Starlit vows, we mean no harm!

A comet zips by with a cheeky grin,
As we whisper sweet nonsense, let the fun begin!
Our love is an indigo mess, quite absurd,
Like cats on a roof, with too many birds.

Beneath constellations, we fumble and trip,
Making indigo dreams with a hapless grip.
Each twinkle a tickle, a cosmic jest,
With laughter our treasure, we're truly blessed.

Flickering Hues of Cherished Bonds

In a canvas of joy, we paint our delight,
With splashes of chuckles that shimmer at night.
Each tickle a color, each grin a shade,
In this comedic art, no glum will invade.

A lettuce green joke, with tomatoes too ripe,
We nourish our bond with a laughing swipe.
Each hue tells a tale, a silly old yarn,
From pumpkin orange pranks to lavender charm.

Flickering moments like candles aglow,
Radiant and silly, we grow and we flow.
In this palette of glee, our hearts play along,
A masterpiece painted with laughter and song.

Canvas of Connection

In a paint shop, we made our pact,
You took blue, and I picked a red.
Mixed together, oh what a fact,
We made a shade no one would tread.

Our love's a blob of mishmash hues,
Splattering laughter, quite out of hand.
Like rainbows turning into blues,
A masterpiece that's less than planned.

With every brush, we bumble and slide,
Like toddlers dancing in a clean room.
A canvas needs a bit of pride,
But we're just crafting chaos and gloom.

Here, let's add some green for kicks,
Just don't ask where the paint went wrong.
In this art we find our tricks,
Connected by laughter all along.

Splashes of Serendipity

You tossed a heart, I threw a wink,
Serendipity, what a silly game!
Our timing's off, but don't you think,
These splashes bring us some sweet fame?

In the park, our picnic's a show,
Mustard spills, oh goodness, what a mess!
But your laughter makes my heart glow,
Let's toast to this too-much-dress!

We hold hands while eating our fries,
Ketchup drips, painted with delight!
Love's not perfect, just like our pies,
Layered with laughter, every bite.

Oh the splashes that decorate fate,
Like paint on a puppy, so divine.
Every moment increases the weight,
Of joy that we twirl on this line.

Glow of Longing

In the glow of our refrigerator light,
I find your face in a slice of cheese.
My heart hums soft in the dead of night,
As I munch away, aiming to please.

Your texts pop like popcorn on the stovetop,
Each message a burst, a hint of a tease.
Longing's a dance that just won't stop,
Like your socks that always aim to seize!

We write our love song with silly rhymes,
Using spaghetti and a dash of flair.
In this kitchen, our style sometimes climes,
To heights of laughter wrapped in shared air.

The glow of longing—it's fun, it's bright,
Like candles melting, making a show.
With every flirty flicker at night,
We discover our hearts are aglow.

Spectrum of Sentiments

In a carnival of quirky hearts,
We ride the highs and float the lows.
Each sentiment is just darts and arts,
With silly lessons that love bestows.

You tickle me in hues of surprise,
My giggles are fireworks in the sky.
With butterflies spun in goofy ties,
In this spectrum, we can't help but fly.

We argue over who's right or wrong,
Like children squabbling over their toys.
But what's a game without laughing along?
Our love's a ruckus, oh how it joys!

So here's to the shades we create,
With every twist, a little flamboyance.
Life's a painting, don't hesitate,
Join me in this colorful dance of brilliance!

Palette of Passion

A red balloon floats by,
With a wink and a sigh.
It giggles as it glides,
Chasing hearts on joyful rides.

In the park, a blue kite flies,
Telling secrets, oh what lies!
It wraps around a tree so tight,
Yelling love with all its might.

Yellow daisies in a row,
Tickling toes, putting on a show.
They dance beneath the sun's bright glare,
Spreading laughter everywhere.

Green frogs leap and croak away,
Singing songs of a funny day.
In the pond, they twirl and twist,
Love is humor, can't be missed.

Shades of Affection

A pink cupcake, frosted sweet,
Whispers, "Date me, I'm a treat!"
With sprinkles popping, oh what fun,
Who knew love could weight a ton?

Orange ties on dancing shoes,
Twirl around, it's good news.
They slip and slide, fall on the ground,
Love's a dance where joy is found.

A purple cat with tiny paws,
Chasing shadows, breaking laws.
It purrs and meows in silly ways,
Bringing laughter to our days.

White clouds puffing, floating high,
Making shapes as they pass by.
One looks like a heart, so round,
In the sky, real love is found.

Tints of Tenderness

A green parrot squawks a tune,
Bumping heads like a cartoon.
It flutters and dances on a branch,
Making love feel like a prance.

A blue fish swims in a bowl,
Teaching hearts how to role.
It blows bubbles of playful glee,
Who knew love could swim so free?

Yellow socks upon the floor,
Were they meant to start a war?
They comically cling, don't let go,
In this chaos, love will flow.

A red scarf caught in a breeze,
Twirling 'round with such great ease.
It tickles noses, makes us laugh,
In this dance, we found our path.

Hues of Heartstrings

A brown dog with floppy ears,
Chases tails and steals our cheers.
With a woof and a playful bark,
Turns the backyard into a park.

Bright gray clouds begin to spill,
Raindrops fall, and hearts get a thrill.
Umbrellas twirl like a happy dance,
In the rain, we give love a chance.

Golden sunflowers stretch up high,
Winking at lovers passing by.
They nod their heads, a bright salute,
Claiming love is so astute.

Lavender fields sway in the breeze,
Sowing laughter among the trees.
Each petal whispers a quiet jest,
In this scene, we truly jest.

Twilight's Caress

A bluebird sings on a purple vine,
Sipping nectar, feeling fine.
He says, "I love her teal eyes bright,"
As they dance in the fading light.

A green frog leaps with silly flair,
Jumping high, without a care.
"I'll wear my bow tie, old and red,"
He croaks, while dreaming of his bed.

Under a sky that's painted pink,
They giggle, share a cupcake stink.
With icing flying, love is grand,
Two hearts marching, hand in hand.

In twilight's glow, with jesting spirits,
Whimsical love, who even hears it?
With playful banter and smiles bright,
Their laughter echoes through the night.

Rich Tones of Togetherness

A purple cat atop a fence,
Winks cheekily, no pretense.
Says to the dog with a wagging tail,
"Together we'll start a grand love tale!"

The dog rolls over with a grin,
Sighs, "Why not, let the fun begin!"
With paws entwined, they start to play,
In a symphony of colors, hip-hip-hooray!

A dash of yellow in their stride,
As they chase rainbows, side by side.
A sprinkle of orange, some laughter too,
Singing silly songs, just me and you.

Their friendship blooms with every hue,
Like a tasty mix of jelly and stew.
In silly antics, love comes alive,
Together in chaos, they happily thrive.

Dappled Dreams

A squirrel spins in a rosy tree,
Chasing dreams, wild and free.
He spots a squirrel with heart-shaped nuts,
Squeaks, "Are those love's secret cuts?"

With acorns rolling, they dash and dart,
In a love chase that's off the chart.
A yellow butterfly flutters near,
Saying, "Your love's as bright as my cheer!"

In dappled sunshine, they laugh and hop,
Wishing their hug will never stop.
A bit of green grass beneath their feet,
Shared giggles, oh, what a treat!

As dusk approaches, colors blend,
With winks and nudges, they pretend.
In dreams of dance, they soar and glide,
Life's whimsical ride, forever side by side.

Fiery Emblems

A cardinal laughs in a flame-like hue,
"Such a fancy suit!" he coos true.
He flits with joy, painting the air,
With a wink he spreads love everywhere!

A grouchy owl hoots, "Don't be a clown!"
But the cardinal dances, wearing a crown.
Together they mix in a tango of cheer,
Spinning tales that all can hear.

A fuchsia flower joins the fun,
With petals bright, they all run.
In a burst of laughter, hearts collide,
In this vibrant swirl, there's nowhere to hide.

With fiery colors and giggles loud,
Two hearts shine, bright and proud.
In the warmth of friendship, forever strong,
In this silly world is where they belong.

Harmonious Hues of Togetherness

In a world of polka dots, we meet,
Your socks are striped, oh what a treat!
With sprinkles on cupcakes, we share a laugh,
Dancing in rainbows, a quirky photograph.

With mustard and ketchup on our lunch plate,
You're the jelly to my peanut—truly great!
Painting the town with mismatched flair,
In the gallery of giggles, we make our lair.

Every rainbow needs its silly end,
Your laughter's the brush, my fondest friend!
We'll color the world in shades of glee,
As we trip on our love, so hilariously.

With crayons unsharpened, we scribble dreams,
Circus of colors, bursting at the seams!
In this artful mess, we take our stance,
Love's a carnival—come join the dance!

The Palette of Yearning Hearts

A palette of wishes, smeared all around,
You say 'I love you' with glittery sound.
Fridge magnets hold notes, wild and bright,
Like two clowns in a car, we're a funny sight!

Your heart's a canvas of polka dots too,
With passion in pink and a dash of blue.
We'll paint the town silly, as wide as the sea,
Turning mundane moments to wild jubilee!

Brushstrokes of laughter mix with our fight,
Like a comedy sketch gone delightfully right.
With splashes of humor and shades of the meek,
We tell our love story, funny, not weak.

So let's swirl the colors, improvise fun,
Underneath starry nights, we'll never quite run.
Our love is a masterpiece, messy yet bold,
With splashes of joy that never get old!

Crimson Pathways of Shared Dreams

Crimson dreams tumble with giggles and schemes,
On pathways of mischief, we burst at the seams.
With each little quarrel, a grin shall arise,
You trip, I trip, it's no big surprise!

In a garden of puns, we dance with delight,
Chasing fireflies in the soft starry night.
Every stumble's a giggle, a twist in our tale,
With ice cream and laughter, we'll never be pale.

When you cast your gaze, the world can't resist,
A rainbow of chuckles wrapped up in a twist.
Two peas in a pod, or maybe a pair,
Of socks that went rogue—what a love affair!

So let's venture forth on this crimson path,
With quirky adventures and delightful math.
Sharing our dreams in a hilariously grand,
Mosaic of laughter, unplanned and unplanned!

The Whisper of Pastel Promises

Whispers of sweetness fill the pastel air,
Like candy floss kisses, beyond compare.
A circus of giggles, you pull my heartstrings,
With balloon animals and misfit flings.

Promises wrapped in ribbons and bows,
Like socks in the dryer, who really knows?
You said you'd cook… Oh dear, what a sight!
Burnt toast and laughter, a culinary fright!

In colors so soft, yet sparkly bright,
We chase after wishes in pure, silly flight.
With soft-spoken jokes that tickle the soul,
Our love's a wild canvas, out of control!

So here's to the whispers and pastel delights,
To the adventurous spirit that ignites our nights.
Hand in hand we'll prance, through laughter and dreams,
In a world full of colors, we'll stitch up our seams!

The Charms of Kaleidoscopic Bonds

In a world of purple pies,
We twirl like dancing fries.
Your laugh's a splash of neon hues,
Mixing joy with silly cues.

Blue balloons in the springtime,
Pop them all, oh what a crime!
Silly love in polka-dot socks,
Tickling hearts like joyful clocks.

With each bouncy pogo stick,
Life's a game, and love's the trick.
Skittles spill across the floor,
Taste of laughter, wanting more!

So grab my hand and let us glide,
On this carnival joyride.
Together we'll make quite a scene,
In our own quirky magazine.

Emblazoned Echoes of Togetherness

With your smile, I'm a wacky kite,
Soaring high in pure delight.
Your wit is like confetti rain,
Colors bursting in my brain.

Tickled by a chocolate sneeze,
We giggle at the silliest tease.
Love's a dance on roller skates,
Falling softly as laughter waits.

Wearing socks that never match,
Playing games with life we catch.
Juggling dreams like clumsy clowns,
Spinning joy through all our towns.

In this whirlwind of delight,
We create our own starlit night.
Each echo of joy, round and round,
Together, we're forever bound.

Twilight's Touch in Burnished Gold

Your hugs are squishy like a sponge,
In twilight's glow, we both plunge.
Sipping tea with giggles bold,
With every cup, our tales unfold.

We wear our quirks like autumn leaves,
Swirling laughter that never leaves.
Jumping puddles in the rain,
Chasing sunshine after pain.

Your jokes are like a playful breeze,
Tickling hearts with perfect ease.
Together we're a vibrant show,
In a circus of hearts aglow.

So let's paint the stars with glee,
In shades of pure jubilee.
With twilight's touch, we'll find our way,
In golden dreams where we can play.

The Serendipity of Starlit Blush

Underneath a polka-dotted sky,
We giggle as the fireflies fly.
Your wink is like a playful wink,
Sparks of joy that make us think.

With marshmallow dreams in the breeze,
We dance like silly bumblebees.
In every whisper and silly fuss,
We spin in circles, just because.

Starlit blush and silly slips,
Your laughter's music to my lips.
We're a pair of running shoes,
Chasing dreams with friendly hues.

So let's create a world so bright,
With colors glowing in the night.
In the serendipity of play,
Love's a prank where hearts do sway.

Melodies in Fuchsia Dreams

In a garden of giggles, we dance and twirl,
Laughing in fuchsia, hearts in a whirl.
A cat with a hat steals a warm croissant,
But in this mad circus, we're far from nonchalant.

A sprinkle of glitter, a dash of delight,
Your jokes hit me funny, like a slap in the night.
With lollipops spiraling, and tulips that grin,
We painted our laughter, let the joy begin!

When jellybeans burst, they tickle my nose,
I trip on my words, and stand on my toes.
Under a candy moon, we bubble and bliss,
Who knew funny feelings could come from a miss?

So here's to our giggles, and all that we share,
In a fuchsia dream, nothing else can compare.
Our hearts are a canvas, bursting with cheer,
With melodies sweet, let's dance like we're here!

The Radiance of Shared Secrets

Whispers like marshmallows, soft and so sweet,
Our giggles in shadows, a hilarious feat.
When you tell a secret with a wink and a grin,
I laugh till I snort; let the fun times begin!

Like two clowns in a circus, our jokes intertwine,
We slip on the punchline, oh, isn't it fine?
Your tales turn to tickles, faced with frothy delight,
In a world painted silly, we're stars of the night.

With cotton candy clouds hovering overhead,
Every silly thought brings laughter instead.
Counting the giggles, we lose track of time,
In a rainbow of secrets, your punchlines rhyme!

So let's share this joy like a treasure we've found,
In this whirl of our laughter, true warmth does abound.
With a wink and a nudge, let's make magic today,
In the radiance found, we'll forever play!

Emerald Echoes of Devotion

In a forest of fun, we skip with pure glee,
Echoes of laughter roll randomly free.
Your green thumb is magic, it tickles the trees,
With mischief as fresh as the buzzing of bees.

A squirrel with sass joins our playful duet,
While we chuckle and chase our dreams without fret.
In leaves made of laughter, we twirl and we sing,
Where emerald moments make my heart take wing!

You paint me with stories, as vivid as spring,
And sway like the branches that sway and swing.
From tangled-up twinkles, our love makes a scene,
In this garden of giggles, we reign like a queen!

So here's to the echoes, both silly and bright,
In this maze of devotion, let's dance through the night.
With emerald bursts shared, let's cherish the fun,
In the forest of laughter, we're never outdone!

The Abyss of Indigo Yearning

In the depths of a night where the indigo shines,
We giggle at shadows and chase silly signs.
With stars that are winking, we jump into dreams,
In this abyss of laughter, humor redeems.

You call out my name in a voice of pure glee,
I trip on my heartstrings like clumsy debris.
With whispers of chaos, we brew strange delights,
In our wild, wacky world, the fun never bites!

A puppy in pajamas plays tag with our sighs,
While moonbeams roll by with their glittery lies.
Each chuckle like bubbles goes floating away,
In the depths of our laughter, we both want to stay.

So in this dark ocean, where humor runs deep,
Let's dance with the swells, take a leap—not a creep!
For in indigo dreaming, we're never apart,
In the abyss of chuckles lies the beat of our heart!

Prismatic Devotion

When she wore blue, I felt so sad,
But red was the shade that drove me mad.
Green made me giggle, yellow was bright,
Like a clown at a party, oh what a sight!

Her heart is a canvas, a riotous spree,
With colors that dance like a playful spree.
Every hue holds a secret or two,
A rainbow of madness, how do you do?

If love were a palette, we'd mix it with glee,
Just watch the wild shades that surface from me.
Together we splash, a colorful fight,
Creating a mural, both funny and bright!

So here's to our canvas, forever it gleams,
With laughter and love, we paint many dreams.
A splash of eccentricity, that's how we flow,
In this whimsical gallery, let's steal the show!

Brushstrokes of Belonging

She said, 'My heart is in a shade of lime,'
I laughed so hard, 'That's simply prime!'
I offered a color called oh-so-fine,
'Let's blend our feelings over a glass of wine.'

His love's a Picasso, a mess in the end,
But I'm the glue, and he's my best friend.
Each brushstroke tickles, as colors align,
Together we paint our own silly design.

Got a splotch of confusion, a drip of delight,
Our palette gets wilder, oh what a sight!
With every mishap, our spirits take flight,
In hues of both laughter, we dance through the night!

So pass me the paint, and we'll throw it around,
Our masterpiece made of giggles profound.
Just don't get it twisted, don't make it unclear,
This canvas we're crafting is full of good cheer!

Luminous Bonds

In the daytime we sparkle, in neon we glow,
With glitter and giggles, our love's quite a show.
When shadows arise, we just laugh them away,
Like fireflies dancing, come join in the play!

His heart shines in colors, like disco lights spin,
Each blink a reminder of where we have been.
We craft our own rhythm, we sing our own tune,
Underneath this vast sky, we sway with the moon.

Every moment's a snapshot, a flash bulb delight,
Captured in colors, oh what a sight!
Like confetti that swirls, we twirl and we dive,
In this carnival of feelings, together we thrive!

So grab your brush, let's paint the night bright,
With hugs like rainbows, our love's outta sight!
In the gallery of laughter, we're both quite a pair,
Creating art from our quirks, beyond compare!

Mosaic of Emotion

Our hearts are like tiles, all mixed up and neat,
With some crazy patterns, they can't be beat!
Each piece tells a story, a dance and a quirk,
As we laugh at the mess — oh, how it can work!

There's a fuchsia of fun, an indigo joke,
With hues that are swirly and just a bit woke.
A splash of confusion, a sprinkle of cheer,
In this dazzling mosaic, together we steer.

So join me, my dear, in this colorful craze,
We'll paint the town silly, in a million ways.
Our love is a puzzle, a riotous blend,
The more that we mix it, the better, my friend!

In each quirk and hue, there's a laugh to be found,
With a brush in our hands, we'll take on the town.
So here's to our mosaic, both crazy and fun,
In this wild art adventure, we're never outdone!

Starlit Wishes in Sapphire

In the night sky, they dance with glee,
A blue balloon floats, just like me.
Wishes are made with a wink and a grin,
Whispers of stars, let the giggles begin.

A silly hat worn by a moonbeam,
Painting the sky with a splattery dream.
Silver laughter bounces, a playful delight,
While comets play peek-a-boo, oh what a sight!

With sprinkles of stardust and a dash of fun,
We chase the glowing fireflies, one by one.
In this sapphire world, where silliness reigns,
We'll laugh till we ache, breaking all chains.

Cotillion of Colors in the Moonlight

A dance of hues in the silver light,
With socks on our hands, we twirl with delight.
Yellow bananas jiggle, pink flamingos sway,
As we hop on one foot, oh what a display!

Cabbage heads dressed in glitter and lace,
Make for a party, a comical grace.
A cake made of sprinkles, not fit for a feast,
Yet everyone laughs, a surreal little beast.

As the moon keeps on chuckling, lights in the sky,
We join in the jig, letting worries fly by.
Our laughter's a rainbow, so bright and so bold,
In this cotillion, our joy won't grow old.

The Opal of Unspoken Affection

In a garden of giggles, where daisies bloom wide,
An opal of joy blooms, love in its stride.
With wobbly legs, a puppy prances near,
Throwing glances like confetti, so pure and sincere.

Beneath all the chatter, there's warmth in the air,
Like a sock running solo, it's a curious pair.
With whispers of whimsy, we dance here and there,
Chasing butterflies that nibble our hair.

And in this odd garden, where silliness reigns,
A bonfire of laughter breaks all the chains.
For the opal in silence speaks loudly, we see,
In the quirky connections, just you and me.

Dusk's Embrace in Warm Amber

Golden light spills as the day takes a bow,
The sun in a hammock, oh what a wow!
Chickens in tutus cluck a funny song,
While crickets do ballet, it won't be long.

A warm amber hug wraps the night in a cheer,
With glowing fireflies as our friends to appear.
Dancing on shadows, under stars we fly,
As tickles of twilight steal half of the sky.

So let's sip our lemonade, add a splash of fun,
We'll toast to the day with all we have done.
In dusk's warm embrace, where laughter will blend,
The night's just beginning; let the frolic not end!

Celestial Colors of Intertwined Souls

In a sky of bright pink fairies,
We juggle oranges and wear blueberries.
Dancing like clowns on a rainbow slide,
Spilling rainbow juice, oh what a ride!

With socks mismatched like our silly game,
We paint our hearts with a dash of fame.
Tickling stars with our goofy grace,
Making comets laugh in endless space.

Each giggle splashes a vibrant hue,
You snort with laughter, and I join too.
Interstellar love like glitter and glue,
While planets spin, our craziness grew.

A canvas stretched under endless skies,
Each splash of laughter, a bright surprise.
Through cosmic winks and wacky twirls,
We're the dizzied dancers of twirled pearls.

Heartbeats in a Sea of Color

In a deep blue sea of jellybean dreams,
We paddle along in vibrant streams.
You shout, 'Shark!' but it's just a fish,
We laugh it off; it's a silly wish!

With hearts doing flip-flops, oh what a sight,
We race from the waves, arms held tight.
Orange octopus playing hide and seek,
In a splash of giggles, it's fun and cheek!

Bubbles tickle our toes with glee,
As dolphins join in our weird jubilee.
Sailing on rainbows, we toss confetti,
Caught in laughter, never feeling petty.

In this colorful whirlpool, we take a dive,
With silly faces, we feel so alive.
Splashing memories as we sail along,
In a sea of joy, where we belong.

The Luminous Journey of Togetherness

On a road paved with candy and ice cream cones,
We trip on gumdrops, spinning like drones.
Our laughter echoes through chocolate trees,
With bubblegum clouds carried by the breeze.

We snort like pigs while walking on stars,
Painting our path, ignoring the cars.
Skipping past rainbows, our shadows dance,
Each goofy step, another chance!

With marshmallow pillows and custard streams,
We bounce on clouds, living our dreams.
In this luminous journey, we trip and fall,
But our taffy hearts stick through it all.

So let's embrace the silly mistakes,
In our colorful world, nothing breaks.
Together forever in giggles we roam,
Through the candyland of our wacky home.

Paintbrush of Elysian Moments

With a paintbrush dipped in fudge and cheer,
We color our world, come over here!
Each drip of laughter, a splash so neat,
Creating joy in a swirl of sweet.

You painted a cat with polka dot glee,
While I twirled colors like a confetti spree.
Splashes of orange with hints of green,
Our masterpiece shines like a goofy dream.

Dancing together on this canvas wide,
We mix up colors with silly pride.
Each brushstroke tells of our laughter's flight,
A whimsical world brought to light.

So grab your colors, and don't be shy,
Let's paint together under the sky.
With each moment, we craft our song,
In this gallery of love, where we belong.

www.ingramcontent.com/pod-product-compliance
Ingram Content Group UK Ltd.
Pitfield, Milton Keynes, MK11 3LW, UK
UKHW030910221224
452712UK00007B/727